Presented to...

_____

With love...

_____

on

_____

God's Wisdom for
Little Boys

Jim & Elizabeth George

Paintings by Judy Luenebrink

HARVEST HOUSE™ PUBLISHERS

EUGENE, OREGON

God's Wisdom for Little Boys

Text copyright © 2002 by Jim & Elizabeth George
Illustrations copyright © 2002 by Judy Luenebrink
Published by Harvest House Publishers
Eugene, OR 97402

Library of Congress Cataloging-in-Publication Data
George, Jim, 1943-
   God's wisdom for little boys / Jim & Elizabeth George; paintings by Judy Luenebrink.
   p. cm.
   Summary: Short verses based on proverbs from the Bible provide examples of how
to live as God wants us to, by doing such things as sharing toys, being friendly, and
helping around the house.
   ISBN-13: 978-0-7369-0824-5
   ISBN-10: 0-7369-0824-2
   1. Boys—Religious life—Juvenile literature. [1. Conduct of life—Biblical teaching.
2. Proverbs.] I. George, Elizabeth, 1944- II. Luenebrink, Judy, ill.
III. Title.
BV4541.3 .G46 2002
248.8'2—dc21   2002001748

Design and production by Matthew Shoemaker

Scripture quotations are from *The International Children's Bible*, New
Century Version, copyright © 1986 by Word Publishing, Nashville,
Tennessee. Used by permission.

Printed in China.

07 08 09 / IM / 15 14

For more information regarding the authors and
illustrator of this book, please contact:

Jim & Elizabeth George
Christian Development Ministries
P.O. Box 2879
Belfair, WA 98528
1-800-542-4611
www.ElizabethGeorge.com

Judy Luenebrink
7057 Hatillo Avenue
Winnetka, CA 91306
1-818-888-9934

To Sean, with love.
You were my inspiration.
—Mom

For Jacob Andrew Seitz

These verses and this book are
written for you, our dear grandson!

May you always seek
God's wisdom.

God's Little Boy

Dear Friend,

There is not a home, church, school, or company in the world that is not in need of men who model godly behavior. Where are these men to be found? They are found in every home where little boys are growing up. Tomorrow's leaders for our churches, our communities, and our world must be trained in our homes today.

May this book of proverbs, so beautifully illustrated by artist Judy Luenebrink, help you to impart God's wisdom to the little boys in your life. May the adventures of "God's Little Boy" assist you in teaching God's truth to your little guys. And may these lively rhymes portray for the next generation what being a godly man is all about.

Yours for the Master,

Jim and Elizabeth

As you begin...

★ ★ ★

Do you like a riddle? Do you like a rhyme?
Then you're going to have a real good time!
A very wise man, a long time ago,
Composed some poems for boys to know.

So hurry! Come on! Drop your things and enjoy
Some virtues and traits of "God's Little Boy."
Discover God's wisdom for boys just like you—
Wisdom to help you your whole life through.

God's Little Boy Is...

Helpful

★ ★ ★

Being helpful is so rare these days!
But God's little boy helps in various ways.
His wonderful service is known near and far,
Like the help he gives in washing the car.

*Whenever you are able,
do good to people who need help.*

Proverbs 3:27

God's Little Boy Is...

Giving

★ ★ ★

Giving to others is always a joy,
Even when giving a favorite toy.
Some folks have plenty but end up poor,
While others give much and end up with more!

A person who gives to others will get richer.
Whoever helps others will himself be helped.

PROVERBS 11:25

God's Little Boy Is...

Wise

★ ★ ★

Do you want to grow up and be a wise man?
Do you want to be smart? God says you can!
Just seek out God's truth throughout your days,
And you'll be wise as you follow His ways.

The mind of a smart person is ready to get knowledge.
The wise person listens to learn more.

PROVERBS 18:15

God's Little Boy Is...

Friendly

★ ★ ★

God's little boy makes friends with others;
Those friends include his sisters and brothers.
True friends are always a gift from above;
Make it your goal to give brotherly love.

A friend loves you all the time.
A brother is always there to help you.

PROVERBS 17:17

God's Little Boy Is...

Hard Working

★ ★ ★

A fool sits around and dreams of plenty,
Failing to rise and work intently.
But a wise little boy works hard and long,
Doing his chores while he hums a song.

The person who works his land will have plenty of food.
But the one who chases useless dreams isn't wise.

PROVERBS 12:11

God's Little Boy Is...

Obedient

★ ★ ★

God teaches children that they should obey
The rules set by others and do what they say.
And God's little boy makes no exceptions—
He always minds and follows directions.

The son who obeys what he has been taught shows he is smart.

PROVERBS 28:7

God's Little Boy Is...

Cheerful

★ ★ ★

It's good to "make a joyful noise,"
Even when made on one of your toys.
A song from your heart helps those who are sad;
It brings a smile and makes them feel glad.

A happy heart is like good medicine.
PROVERBS 17:22

God's Little Boy Is...

Truthful

★ ★ ★

Have you ever done wrong and wanted to lie,
Thinking a story will help you get by?
Telling the truth is what God says to do.
So always be sure you say what is true.

Don't use your mouth to tell lies.
Don't ever say things that are not true.

PROVERBS 4:24

God's Little Boy Is...

Thrifty

★ ★ ★

"A penny saved is a penny earned,"
This is a fact that should be learned.
Saving your pennies helps with your needs
And gives you extra for many kind deeds.

Money that comes easily disappears quickly.
But money that is gathered little by little will slowly grow.

PROVERBS 13:11

God's Little Boy Is...

Brave

★ ★ ★

What can you do to be fearless and strong,
To be bold and brave your whole life long?
You don't need to worry or be afraid,
For God has promised to come to your aid!

You won't need to be afraid when you lie down.
When you lie down your sleep will be peaceful.
...The Lord will keep you safe.

PROVERBS 3:24,26

God's Little Boy Is...

Self-Controlled

★ ★ ★

If you fail to learn to hold yourself back,
And let yourself go and get out of whack,
You'll be like this castle, once so grand,
Whose walls fall down when waves hit the sand.

*A person who does not control himself
is like a city whose walls have been broken down.*

PROVERBS 25:28

God's Little Boy Is...

Disciplined

★ ★ ★

Folks who love to stay in bed
Miss the thrills of the day ahead.
God's little boy gets up at dawn,
Happy to help 'til the day is gone.

The lazy person is like a door that turns back and forth on its hinges.
He stays in bed and turns over and over.

PROVERBS 26:14

Smile
Clean
Room
Walk
Dog
Feed
Frog
Be
Thankful

M T W Th F Sa Su

JOURNAL

Bible
DOG
TALES

All Star

God's Little Boy Is...

Diligent

★ ★ ★

Diligent men spend their time and their days
Doing their work in various ways.
The same thing is true of God's little guy.
Oh, boy! Soon there will be apple pie!

The person who works his land will have plenty of food.
But the one who chases useless dreams instead will end up very poor.

PROVERBS 28:19

God's Little Boy Is...

Kind

★ ★ ★

"I love being kind," says God's little boy,
"Giving to others and bringing them joy."
Now, how about *you*? What can *you* share?
What can *you* do to show people *you* care?

Don't ever stop being kind and truthful.
Let kindness and truth show in all you do.

PROVERBS 3:3

God's Little Boy Is...

Content

★ ★ ★

When you go outside and you're still as can be,
And you take time to notice, to hear, and to see,
Then all of the wonders that God made for you
Will bring peace of mind and contentment, too.

Peace of mind means a healthy body.

PROVERBS 14:30

God's Little Boy Is...

Industrious

★ ★ ★

A boy can do many things with his time;
He can waste it…or spend it using his mind.
Better it is when the day is done
To have learned, and grown, and had some fun!

Those who work hard make a profit.
But those who only talk will be poor.

PROVERBS 14:23

God's Little Boy Is...

Responsible

★ ★ ★

When something or someone means something to you,
There's no task so hard that you wouldn't do.
A responsible person makes sure to attend
To taking good care of his things and his friend.

Be sure you know how your sheep are doing.
Pay close attention to the condition of your cattle.

PROVERBS 27:23

WATER

God's Little Boy Is...

Thankful

★ ★ ★

Thank You, dear God, for blessing me—
With food, a home, and a family.
And now, O Lord, I ask if You might
Help me be honest and do what is right.

The Lord…is pleased with an honest person's prayer.
The Lord…hears the prayers of those who do right.

PROVERBS 15:8,29

God's Little Boy Is...

Prayerful

★ ★ ★

The Bible's best wisdom for all little boys
Is not to want treasures of trinkets and toys!
Instead God says you're simply to cling
More to the Lord than to any thing.

Dear God above, for this I pray—
To be a godly man someday.
Make me a man who loves You true,
A man of wisdom who pleases You.

Wisdom begins with respect for the Lord. And understanding begins with knowing God, the Holy One.

PROVERBS 9:10

Words to Know

★ ★ ★

The Word	What It Means
rhyme	words that sound alike
composed	put words together in a story or song
virtues	the good things about a person
traits	the way a person acts and talks
wisdom	use the mind in a good and right way
various	different kinds
intently	to do something really well
exceptions	something different than what is normal
out of whack	get out of proper order or shape
diligent	a hard worker
contentment	happy and thankful for what you have
responsible	doing what you should do
honest	to tell the truth
trinkets	something small with little or no value